DICK ADAIR'S
SAIGON

DICK ADAIR'S

Sketches and

SAIGON

Words from the Artist's Journal

with a foreword by PETER ARNETT

WEATHERHILL

New York · Tokyo

To
FRED AND KAZ HARRIS
who shared the wine

FIRST EDITION, 1971

Published by John Weatherhill, Inc., 149 Madison Ave, New York, New York 10016, with editorial offices at 7-6-13 Roppongi, Minato-ku, Tokyo 106, Japan. Copyright in Japan, 1971, by John Weatherhill, Inc.; all rights reserved. Printed in Japan.

LCC CARD NO. 78-157268
ISBN 0-8348-0062-4

CONTENTS

FOREWORD

by Peter Arnett

WARS RAKE across human history. They have been fought with long bows and atom bombs, in frozen mountains and sweating fields. Millions have died anonymously as the bloody tides of history ebb and flow.

On occasion someone has been along to record these bloody events for posterity, to illuminate this dark side of man. And so it is with Vietnam. The world is well aware of the thoroughness with which chroniclers have recorded this Southeast Asian war: the millions of words, the streams of wirephotos, the miles of television tapes, the radio broadcasts. On volume, Vietnam is said to have been the most well-covered war in history.

Some press critics have said the war was overcovered. Certainly, as the Indochina conflict entered the decade of the seventies the world, if not completely buried in Vietnam copy, was bored. Mention Vietnam in America and you could hear the click of minds closing on the subject across the country.

But wars just don't go away, they end. And until they do they fascinate mankind because of the forces they unleash. And even afterwards when the killing stops and nature begins her healing processes on shattered lives and devastated countryside, the memory of the war remains, indelible on

history. We remember the Thirty Years' War and not the fifty years of peace that followed, and so it is through history.

I contributed to the endless flow of Vietnam War copy for eight years. But I am not defensive about the press role nor embarrassed by the quantity of coverage that spilled out over the years. Too much cannot be written about any war if only in the hope that in some future time the grim catalogue gathered through centuries of warfare might at last persuade man to forego it entirely.

The factor overlooked by the Vietnam War strategists was the people, the anonymous millions who lived on the bloodied battlefields or fled panic-stricken to the doubtful safety of the cardboard cities.

It is the Vietnamese people that artist Dick Adair captures in the sketches in this book, and looking over copies of the sketches and text from his publisher as I sit writing this foreword in New York City on a cold winter day, I feel myself again walking the sweating streets of Saigon, gagging on the putrid air and sidestepping the vendors whose sidewalk supermarkets sprawl into the gutters.

Dick Adair captures many qualities in his sketches. One that shines through particularly for me is the endurance of the Vietnamese; the peasant woman fleeing from a

7

street battle, her child clutched in her arms, her body bent forward in strain, her face screwed up less in fear than in determination to save her loved one. Or the knowing leer of the street urchin relaxing on the pavement as he sizes up his next mark, maybe the well-heeled American construction worker in town for a binge, or the downy-faced group of GIs sneaking a look at the wicked city before heading back into the spartan life in the jungles.

The Vietnamese need this quality of endurance. They have an incredibly greedy appetite for war. The 1970s saw the start of their fourth decade of virtually continuous conflict. An estimate indicates that one thousand people have died violently each week in the three previous decades. There were slow months in those thirty years when a sort of dubious peace seemed to prevail across the land. But those few halcyon days have been sharply redressed by the frequent bloodlettings that have burst into newspaper headlines and exposed Vietnam as a raw nerve in the body politic of the world.

The 1968 Tet Offensive that smashed through South Vietnam's cities and towns may well have been the Dien Bien Phu of the Second Indochina War. And this blunt comparison to the military debacle that ended French hopes in Indochina is valid and important in that it indicates that the climactic battle of the Vietnam War had been fought, that it was an irrevocable setback to Western hopes, and that it persuaded the United States dramatically to alter its goals in Indochina. I believe the war is still regarded as incidental by the men behind the communist curtain, a necessary diversion from the main struggle to dominate the broad mass of the population.

The departure of the American army from Vietnam does not mean that the agony in Vietnam will end. It will undoubtedly continue.

Across the centuries the Vietnamese have displayed an infinite capacity for waging war among themselves. The American presence has not been decisive. The departure of the Americans in the early 1970s promises only to reduce the scope of the war, not to end it. Vows from both sides to continue fighting already guarantee bloody conflict for possibly a decade more—the time some see as necessary for final victory for one side or the other.

Still, while the Vietnamese people have shown an uncomplaining willingness to fight these past three decades of war, the continuing propulsion comes from a narrow group of extremist leaders on both sides for whom there is no middle way. There is always the possibility that the masses will declare a plague on both houses and seek a middle course despite the most vigorous objections of entrenched leadership. But this middle course would probably only be achieved after much more bloodshed. The prognosis for sick Vietnam as it entered its fourth decade of tumult was for more of the same.

*   *   *

Artist Dick Adair wandered into this tropical buzzsaw innocently seeking adventure and an opportunity to use his knack for sketching, a knack he developed under the famous artist-correspondent John Groth at the Art Students League in New York. He found adventure enough, but until this book he mostly hid his sketching talent in notebooks stuffed into the false walls of a *Playboy*-style pad decored with a circular bed and an indoor waterfall he designed for himself in the heart of Saigon.

He designed other gorgeous places in Vietnam, gracing remote, dusty American army field installations with gaily decorated club houses to relieve the monotony of the soldiers, or indulging himself in more prosperous Saigon where he came up with a splendid trolley-car-like drinking place that immediately became famous.

Dick was making a good living this way, but his heart remained faithful to the purpose that had pulled him to Vietnam in the first place: to draw the war. I used to encounter him occasionally in a Tu Do bar, or flying out to Hong Kong, and he would express his longing to give up all his business, don fatigues, and draw the war. But he looked so brightly intelligent and prosperous that I figured he was putting me on. That was until I took him up on a longstanding invitation to visit his playboy pad, and saw his sketches.

Dick has the rare, amazing facility to catch the spirit of his subject with extraordinary economy of line. His sketches throb with action. He calls them "gesture drawings" and they show his Saigon—the bar girls, the street people, the laborers, and scores of others, ordinary and extraordinary.

I was eager to have him draw the war for the Associated Press, and we planned forays together into the field. I knew his sketches would superbly supplement our news stories and photographs of the war. They would give added insight and depth. But we never did go out together because the best laid plans in Vietnam were always upset by some overriding development. But while his sketching may have been lost to the Associated Press, it has at last been made available in this volume.

Dick did eventually get out to the war in the countryside, as the sketches at the end of this book show. These are well done, but to me his best works are his Saigon sketches. They seem to burst with the life of the streets, possibly because he was drawing most of them purely for fun and unpressured by deadlines. In them he has caught the cruelly selfish bar hostesses with the paddy mud still on their knees, queens for a war-torn city that allowed itself to be too easily corrupted. And here too are the black marketeers straddling the streets, one eye cocked for the bribe-hungry Saigon police, the other for the street kids who can snatch a box of PX soap off the blanket and disappear up an alley like water flushed through a toilet. And there are hundreds of other familiar characters. Dick sketched them on the spot, on the backs of bills of lading, on invoices, bar coasters, and sometimes a sketch pad. He once told me that as a designer he built all kinds of bar stools but that his real pleasure was sitting in Mimi's Bar and sketching the way some construction worker's bulk draped around a bar stool in a way that revealed he was bored.

Much of Dick's Saigon sketching must have been therapeutic, to give some intellectual depth to the one-dimensional scenes he lived with, one dimensional because a foreigner soon found in Saigon that he was not permitted to penetrate deeper than the outer layer of society. There was another dimension to it, too. Dick was pestered by a grotesque leper who took it upon himself to watch all cars parked on a street near the Caruso restaurant, a favorite gathering place. Dick sketched him from memory one night and as though he had cast some voodoo spell he never saw the leper again. "I tried to exorcise some of my competition the same way, but it never quite worked again," he recalls sadly.

Dick Adair's book of sketches then is not directly concerned with the Vietnam War; it shows us instead reflections of the war. To my mind these reflections are as necessary to understanding the nature of that conflict as the war itself. It was from the teeming streets of Saigon and other major cities that the communists recruited and plotted their most successful and auda-cious acts. The characters peopling this book—the cyclo drivers, refugees, whores, monks, street kids, cops, soldiers, black-marketeers, and POWs—reveal the faces that frustrated the best and most ardent intentions of the West in Vietnam. And more than that, the atmosphere of a nation at war is superbly captured here. For anyone who has ever lived in Saigon these vividly drawn sketches revive sharply and accurately the bittersweet flavor of the years just past.

PROLOGUE

IN EARLY MAY, 1965, the freighter *President Adams* steamed cautiously into crowded Yokohama Bay, the first stop on a round-the-world voyage. In the driving rain the pilot and the captain could barely see through the bridge windows. Between strokes of the wiper blades they could just make out the oilskin-clad figure of the ship's carpenter as he struggled to the forepeak to tend the anchor. It was a simple task, one the veteran seaman had done hundreds of times.

But this time his rubber boots betrayed the carpenter's old sea legs. For just as he reached the top of the forepeak ladder, he slipped, his legs lurched aft and his body fell forward and, missing his grip on the slippery railing, the old man hit his chin on the topmost rung and proceeded to count each succeeding rung thereafter down to the maindeck, his head nodding all the way as if in grotesque approval, until he settled at the bottom in a heap of oilskins.

The ship's captain was too much of a seasoned seaman to indulge himself in more than a sigh and a passing remark to the pilot that it looked as if it were going to be "one of those kind of voyages." Then he calmly ordered the first mate to have the dayman rescue the carpenter and tend to the anchor.

I never met the old carpenter (who was sent to a hospital ashore with a broken jaw), but I did know the dayman who took his place, and the able-bodied seaman watchstander who became the dayman, and the ordinary seaman who moved up to the able-bodied slot. Because I was the ordinary seaman who took the ordinary's place.

The berth on the *President Adams* could not have come at a better time. For more than a year I had wandered around Japan as a freelance artist. But my real ambition was somehow to break into print as an artist-correspondent, and so I dug into my dwindling resources to pay for a round-trip ticket to Taiwan, where I sketched the Nationalist Chinese Army on the island of Quemoy hoping that my work would attract the attention of editors and lead to future assignments.

The sketches did win me some attention, but whether the assignments would have been forthcoming or not I'll never know. The trip left me broke and I was about to indenture myself to pay off my bar bills when the old carpenter's accident left an opening that I was happy to fill.

I had mixed feelings as I climbed the *Adams'* gangway that spring morning. In spite of this fortunate reprieve from poverty, I was, in fact, giving up and being repatriated just short of getting started in my chosen profession.

The American build-up hadn't yet begun at that time, but Vietnam was where

Old sailor climbing to bridge

the action was. I had gone to Quemoy to prove my sketching talent under fire, but it was no secret among my friends in Tokyo that I wanted somehow to make my way to Vietnam. Now, after brief stops at Okinawa, Keelung, and Hong Kong, the *Adams* was making its way cautiously up the Saigon River to unload military cargo. According to the ship's schedule I could look forward to a mere three days in Vietnam, and that as a seaman. It was a sad irony.

The Continental Palace Hotel, located just off Lam Son Square in a downtown section of Saigon, is popular for strolling in and meeting friends. I was sitting on the hotel's open terrace nursing a gin and tonic when an old Japan friend, Frank Kernan, passed by. Frank was overjoyed with the money he was making—he'd known some lean days in Tokyo—working for Raymond-Morrison-Knudsen (RMK), the giant construction firm that was doing most of the military building in Vietnam.

That same day Frank introduced me to the RMK personnel manager, who informed me that although they desperately needed help he could not guarantee me a job even if I returned to Saigon after my ship completed its voyage. The whole operation might be closed down by then, he warned, depending on what kind of decision Congress made.

Frank consoled me and offered to put me up at his house if the company was still hiring in a few months and, just as important, if I had the money to make it back to Saigon. The next morning the *Adams*, with me aboard, left for Singapore.

A day out of Saigon the sea began to rise and once again fate moved in my favor at the expense of another. This time it was the mate on my watch whose stomach reacted from the rolling ship now light after discharging the bulk of its cargo in Vietnam. So, while the captain himself stood bridge watch that night I was at the wheel, and I couldn't resist the opportunity to tell him my story.

My problem had to do with the ship's articles, the nautical contract that governs sailors at sea. The articles of American ships state that a seaman cannot leave ship in a foreign port without the captain's written consent, which must be witnessed by the U. S. consul in port. The articles also

Vietnamese mother and child

state that no ship may leave a port under-manned. The situation, as I presented it, clearly left my destiny in the hands of the captain as to whether I would have a career at sea or ashore. Whether my performance on deck influenced the captain or not I'll never know, but he had no objections to my leaving the ship providing I was able to find a replacement.

For a replacement I found a bearded hippie living in a Sikh temple near the American embassy in Singapore. He'd drifted to the Orient working on foreign ships and was now living on small doles from the embassy. He was very happy to become the ordinary to replace the ordinary who replaced the ordinary, etc., and I even threw into the deal a pair of rubber boots because his sandals might prove slippery and lead to a repeat performance on the forepeak ladder.

The next morning the captain, the purser, the hippie, the consul, and I all met. It was agreed that the hippie could keep his long hair but his pet monkey had to go. Reluctantly the hippie turned Snyder, his monkey, over to me demanding that I promise to let him listen to bongo music

occasionally. Snyder loved bongos. As a final gesture I handed over my rubber boots to complete the ceremony.

I didn't have enough money for the round-trip ticket to Saigon which is necessary in order to acquire a Vietnamese visa. But I was able to exchange Snyder for a letter of guarantee written to the Vietnamese embassy by the pretty Malayan girl who works in the travel bureau at Singapore's Adelphe Hotel, and who also has an affinity for bongos. Thus I was able to get my entry visa.

Frank was more than a little surprised to see the ex-seaman at his door only four days after he had offered his hospitality. Both of us were relieved when RMK hired me a few days later.

For the next three months I worked at the port supervising the unloading of military cargo. At the end of that time I was unhappy to find that my creative efforts had been limited to messing up a lot of cargo delivery sheets with random sketches and to stuffing French bread with ham, cheese, and tomatoes from the *assiette anglaise* at the Catinat Hotel, thereby introducing the submarine sandwich to Saigon.

Balloon seller

So I gave notice to RMK and was prepared to use my savings to support myself in the field. But, then, through a friend, the late Al Ricketts, entertainment columnist for *Stars & Stripes*, I was approached by a local military supply company to head their design department for the construction of military clubs. A good opportunity, I thought, to get closer to the war while still remaining a respectable member of the foreign business community.

The side of the war I was exposed to over the next four and a half years had very little to do with the battlefield scenes I wanted to draw. Instead I earned a reputation for transforming tents, barrack huts, rooftops, French villas and patios into makeshift imitations of plush Stateside lounges and "niteries." Sometimes, though, at outlying bases I saw weary troops returning by helicopter from patrols and small battles. This experience was like sitting in a locker room watching the players shuffle in

and wondering what the game had been like.

But most of my time was spent in Saigon. I stayed in the city and the war was outside, though not so far that I could not indulge in the late evening pastime of sitting in the lounge atop the Majestic Hotel and watching armed helicopters firing on suspected Viet Cong positions across the river. Down in the street the people seemed oblivious to any activity other than their own languid movements. Occasionally a breeze came off the river carrying the smell of oil and rotting refuse, but beyond the great cathedral at the head of Tu Do Street hardly a leaf would stir except from the heat that rose from the pavement. Everywhere the air was thick with the sickening sweet smell of decaying fruit and flowers. Those among the passersby who weren't rummaging through the garbage piled in the streets didn't seem to be at all concerned that it was there, probably because the

Rounding up Viet Cong suspects during the Tet Offensive

stench had become part of the neighborhood atmosphere. Back in the alleys the doors and windows of the wooden houses and plaster shacks were wide open. You could look in and see the laundry drying, hear the radios, and smell the fermented-fish sauce cooking on open burners.

In spite of the dirt and foul odors it was a great place to draw. I had acquired a perverse fascination for the baroque detail in French wrought-iron balconies, crowded sidewalks, and rotting garbage. But I was still not drawing the war—the men under fire, the war that Peter Arnett was writing about and Horst Faas was photographing. The action was in the field and it didn't look like I'd ever make it there. And then one day the war came to Saigon.

Tet, the Lunar New Year, is the most festive occasion of the Vietnamese year. It is everybody's birthday, Christmas, and New Year's all rolled into a grand eight days of merry making. Nguyen Hue becomes the "Street of Flowers" and all traffic is stopped to make way for flower vendors and toy peddlers. For more than a week the city explodes with firecrackers from morning to night, culminating in a final day-long blowout when even curfew is suspended.

On January 31, 1968, when the revelers began to get into the swing of the season, the Viet Cong attacked Saigon. Fear swept through the streets, silencing the celebrators. All civilian traffic stopped, and the streets became deserted. Houses and stores were shut up tight and families huddled together and waited. Outside, armored vehicles raced unhindered through intersections that had been jammed with Tet revelers only hours before. The streets had never been so quiet and an eerie tension gripped everyone so that heads jerked and nerves quivered at the mere slam of a door. The usually languid Vietnamese became abrupt and jerky in their movements like comic characters from a silent film. Even those who composed themselves well spoke in voices an octave higher than usual.

There were no firecrackers now and not the slightest doubt that the sound of small-arms fire was the real thing. When street fighting broke out and fires razed whole neighborhoods, people fled into the streets carrying their children and possessions. Before the battle was over, thousands of

Street of bars

people had been killed and many more were wounded and homeless.

It was many months before things began to return to normal. Business resumed but somehow the city had changed and I never saw it as it was before the Tet Offensive, though I remained there for two and a half more years.

The shooting and the killing were no longer just items in the morning newspaper. They were real. Bars were shut down and all cabarets were forced to close their doors. But before long the bar and cabaret owners found ways to circumvent the new laws. With that the authorities chose to enforce a wartime austerity law and soon it was against the law to dance, even in one's own home.

The city was changed, but my routine continued pretty much the same. Over the years I sketched almost constantly. I sketched, in one sense, much for the same reason a mental patient paints—therapeutically. The drawings I produced are my statements, my complaints about the heat, the price of Saigon tea, and the indifference of the whores. They are also a record of an important part of my life.

While life in the city had its unforgetta-ble moments, it was more often monotonous. Then, like thousands of other members of Saigon's foreign community, I sought diversion in back-alley bars and bistros, went on picnics and outings to safe areas, threw lavish parties, and looked about for new kinds of entertainment. Sketching the life of the city was one such diversion. If most of what I experienced was not the war, it certainly showed the reflections of war.

In 1969, just prior to a new enemy offensive on Special Forces camps near the Cambodian border, John Baker, then managing editor of the *Stars & Stripes,* made arrangements for me to go out in the field on special assignment as a fully accredited artist-correspondent. The following week I picked up my press passes, fatigue uniforms, and jungle boots, and jammed my baggy knee pockets with sketch pads.

I spent the first two weeks at the Special Forces camp at Duc Lap, where I sketched between bouts of enemy shelling. A short while later I went out on a patrol with soldiers from Delta Troop, 1st Squadron, 10th Cavalry in which 4,500 pounds of enemy rice were confiscated. Before returning to Saigon, I made a visit to a Montagnard village just outside Pleiku where I sketched the members of a Civilian Irregular Defense Group. The scenes I saw with these outfits also became part of my Vietnam record.

With the field duty under my belt, my Vietnam "assignment" was complete. I sketched very little action other than what had come almost to my doorstep. I recorded instead the life of the capital of a nation at war, the ordinary citizens and the foreign community, the stevedores and shopkeepers, campworkers, and cyclo drivers, peddlers, beggars, lepers, mothers and children, old women, idlers, whores, street kids, Buddhist monks, VC prisoners of war, ARVN soldiers and GIs, and the traffic cop on the corner. In short, all that I observed and was involved with. This book, then, is a testament of my sojourn in Vietnam in the years 1965 to 1970.

Port of
Saigon

AT THE DOCKS

A TUG MANEUVERS the freighter to the dock and with two blasts of its whistle announces that we are in place. Heaving lines fly through the air and thud heavily on the dock. Frail Vietnamese dockworkers grab them and struggle to haul the clumsy manila line from the water as the ship's aftergang waits impatiently. At last the dockworkers get the loop around the bollard and we crewmen take the turns to the winch that draws the ship to the dock.

Lines are rapidly made secure, rat guards fixed in place, the gangway lowered. Then up come the people from customs, quarantine, and the ship's agent. The landing is official. We are in Saigon.

The watch leans over the dockside rail, running a skeptical eye over the Vietnamese stevedores who are sluggishly making their way up the gangplank. They are skinny little men, half-naked in striped droopy drawers or loincloths, and listless women in baggy black pantaloons. Each carries a few pieces of French bread wrapped in newspaper, and rice for lunch in little tin buckets.

The stevedores ease into their jobs. Pontoons are lifted from the hatch in a way that seems needlessly complicated to the restlessly watching crew. Before long the mate is blowing his top. The hold is open, but fully a third of the stevedores are hunkering on the crates and sucking on bamboo pipes. This sluggishness runs against the

Off-loading a freighter

Waiting for a heaving line from the ship

American grain. But this is Vietnam and that is how Vietnamese stevedores work the hold.

The sun is scorching hot now and the steel deck can blister bare feet. That's why they're up on the crates, somebody explains. The mate, however, is not to be put off. He mutters that if they're going to just squat on their skinny haunches, they can at least obey fire regulations and put out those goddamn weird pipes.

The work progresses. Reefer doors long closed are pried open and steel-banded meat cartons are passed from hand to hand to be restacked on the already slung pallets. Looking at the underfed workers, you hope that a pallet will fall, a carton break, that a liberated steak will keep fresh in the heat of a woman's baggy pants till she can get it home. Rice is easier to steal. A deft jab with the grappling hook and it pours out on the hold deck like Morton's salt. That way they don't have to pack it in their pants till they're cleaning the hold in the last ten minutes before work ends.

Out on deck the watch is puzzled about

Harbor scene, Port of Saigon

Off-loading cargo from the hold

why it takes two men to work the winches, one man to each handle. But the left seems to know what the right is doing and the hook carries the pallet over the side and lays it fairly accurately on a flatbed truck.

An American supervisor starts in bitching because the pallets are not all facing the same way. Then another supervisor is heard complaining in the yard that his men can't get their forks under the loads. This same American will curse his smiling driver six or seven times a day for misjudging the height of the forks and ramming them into an expensive piece of equipment.

Another time you'll see him turn beet red in the sun as he wipes the sweat of frustration from his brow and fumes because the Vietnamese driver can't understand what he means by "Stop riding the goddamn clutch!"

Somehow though the work gets done— in the Vietnamese way, languidly.

WATERFRONT SKETCHES

Dockworker tying up ship

When I could steal the time, I sketched. Like I'd ride off on a forklift, pretending I was going to check pallets. But at the dock I'd stop before a ship off-loading rice and I'd sketch the longshoremen struggling with the slings, trying to catch the lines of their movements before I became obvious.

Hunkering stevedore

Aftergang working the winch

Port of Saigon, ships berthed bow to stern

Woman stevedore resting

Foreman and stevedore

Crewmen watch activity in the hold

Stevedore sitting one out

The watch acts as security in the hold

The Yard

Inside the RMK yard

Laborers loading cement on truck

*Laborers waiting
for work orders*

RMK ALL THE WAY

THE TIME IS JUNE, 1965. President Johnson hasn't yet announced the big military build-up for Vietnam. Air Marshall Ky has been in power for a only few months, but his hard-line policy on demonstrators and those of questionable loyalty offers new confidence to resident Americans. They think they can see Ky's determination reflected in shopkeepers and laborers and so they have become less patient with waiters who still insist on affecting a French attitude of indifference.

Port of Saigon, where I worked for three months, is an overcrowded staging area for military equipment. Cargo is off-loaded from ships by soldiers, sailors, and American and Vietnamese civilians, all trying to use the cramped, far-too-small working area to accommodate both trucks and cargo. The traffic is ridiculous. Thirty-ton flatbed trucks become snarled among great piles of barbed wire, crates, tires, and stacks of steel. As the staging area grows bigger the roads in it get smaller. Every driver is convinced that he has the right of way and as often as not it's the hapless ninety-five-pound Vietnamese driver who bears the brunt of the curses as he tries to maneuver an overloaded truck.

The civilians who stage the cargo for RMK aren't all from the ranks of those professional hardhats who migrate from one international worksite to another. Many are Americans who have made their way to Saigon after working at odd jobs in Korea and Japan. The lure of a thousand dollars a month plus two hundred seventy-five living allowance, tax free, fills the company's call for manpower. Others who come are Australians and Filipinos—called "third nationals"—who do the same work but receive less pay, based on the living standard of their countries.

As civilians we seem to be an isolated activity in the midst of military logistics. There is resentment among the GIs, and fights frequently break out over control of hot plates and coffee urns. These are days reminiscent of the gold rush, an obvious image to a good number of GIs who take their discharge here and return to their old warehouses as highly paid hardhats.

There are rumors of a build-up and others of a withdrawal. The threat of being laid off doesn't seem to concern us as much as where we will put everything if shipping increases. Even now more and more ships are winding their way up the Saigon River. Before docking many of them will have to turn around at the Catinat Pier at the base of Tu Do Street in full view of the My Canh Floating Restaurant, site of the most recent and most terrible of terrorist attacks on the city. To American seamen it seems as though they are being paraded before the scene as a reminder of why they are earning double wages.

I soon learn that a storekeeper's duties

With the shortage of men
women take on the heavy
labor, adding a touch
of glamour to the scene

aren't anything like what the job title suggests. What I do is supervise the unloading of trucks that bring cargo from the ships by yelling at the Vietnamese laborers in English and corrupt French. Then the problem is for me to remember where I've piled the supplies until I can find another truck to move them out of the yard.

There is already a Vietnamese checker who keeps track of the cargo. But I'm supposed to keep track of him and just so he understands my superiority, I'm encouraged to carry a large authoritative-looking clipboard. On it I keep a ream of blank cargo-delivery forms which are fine for sketching. I look very busy, especially when George, the port supervisor, comes around.

I was a little slow the first week on the job, but as soon as I kicked the Kaopectate habit I was able to expand the radius of my working area and discover unchartered staging space. George always wore a scowl on his face as if he didn't like the taste of the tobacco in his pipe. Later I learned that he continually suffered from the same malady

I had had the first week and was himself confined to an area within six minutes of the john. I guess that's why he walked so fast in the tropic heat. For a while there I thought he was just trying to impress everybody with a sense of urgency.

It wasn't until the first 25,000 American troops were officially committed that the top blew off in the yard. Suddenly there were new faces everywhere. Some with helmets. These were the real pros, easily recognized by their uniform: hard hats, field boots, and colorful aloha shirts. They were called foremen and had red noses and demanded company cars with drivers. I knew they were veterans of many foreign jobs because they began yelling at everybody their first day in the yard.

I felt we were really coming into the big time. Now there were at least two Americans and a Filipino to yell at the forklift driver, who was strangely unimpressed and still managed to place the forks above the pallet and ram them into the cargo.

Somehow all the added advice didn't create what was really (continues on page 39)

Cement carriers unloading a truck

Cement is always in demand in Vietnam and at the yard we handled plenty of it. In every load some sacks are torn. These were turned over to the women who pour it through funnels into new sacks. The eyes of the cement carriers suffer from the dust, and each sack bears a distinctive stain from the sweat that also streaks their dust-covered faces.

At night the dust hangs in the air above the high piles of cement like an eerie mist. Ghostly white laborers shoulder the bags and pass them tier by tier to the tops of the piles. Off to the side women sit about sewing torn sacks, talking and spitting red betel juice, their mouths like gaping wounds.

Laborers who have escaped the
draft are generally frail
and spindly, and the heavy
labor sometimes makes agonizing
demands on their strength

needed—more space to stage the cargo. In fact, with all the new guys standing around there was less room than before.

The Vietnamese were not particularly inspired by all the new supervision since they knew it took only a certain amount of labor to unload a truck, and the yard could only hold a certain number of trucks—if there ever were enough to go around. So the Vietnamese who weren't working at the moment continued to hunker in the shade and watch us get sunburned.

Unskilled workers were our biggest problem. They were mostly tubercular old men or young boys. Those who were really useful came within the draft age and only escaped the army's clutches because they were blind in one eye or were the sole sup-

Women laborers salvaging spilled cement

Yard workers

Vietnamese names were troublesome in the beginning, though with a little effort anyone could remember and pronounce them passably well. There is one Vietnamese name which I never have trouble remembering. One day the clerk who made out the bills of lading that were to accompany each truck made an error that I didn't discover until the truck was well on its way. It was the end of a hot, frustrating day and I exploded and cursed him out, using some choice expressions. He didn't understand all I was saying, but he caught one word in particular. When I let up for a moment, he smiled sheepishly and said, "No, sir. Phūc . . . my name is Phūc."

port of five or more kids (who were sometimes borrowed from the neighbors). Even at that, Marshall Ky's airplanes continually showered our maimed and spindly labor force with leaflets urging our patriots to rally to the cause.

Then came the rains. And did it rain! It suddenly became obvious why the U.S. Army had given this portion of the port to the civilian firms. The flooding was so bad an LST could have sailed right up to the warehouse. At the first downpour the guard shack floated away. The guards were bearded and turbaned Sikhs and former Gurkhas, proud veterans of Her Majesty's Army who remained undaunted and navigated their garrison back to its former position. The forklift driver, however, showed no inclination to go down with his machine and would abandon ship at the first boom of thunder.

Monsoon rains are unpredictable. Skies can turn black in three directions though not a drop of rain will fall. At other times a slender streak of dark gray comes sneaking over the warehouse roof at low altitude and within minutes we're battling the tides again. The storms end as quickly as they come, and even more remarkable is how fast the sun sucks up everything but the mud in half an hour. Even George learned not to throw out his soggy tobacco the few times his long-practiced quickstep failed him.

Newly hired yard workers just in from the country

When he catches a goof-off like this guy, the ordinary supervisor will begin chewing him out immediately. But if the supervisor is an artist, he'll quietly sketch him first—and then jump down his throat.

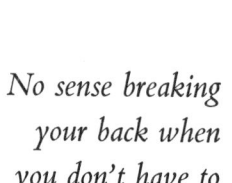

No sense breaking your back when you don't have to

A DEATH IN THE YARD

ONE DAY AN explosion rocked the yard and a small ominous-looking cloud of smoke rose above the machine shop. Several of our Vietnamese workmen had been welding a fuel tank without properly purging it. The blast killed one man and several others were injured. Everyone rushed to the scene and some of the laborers, more daring than the rest, crept around to peer under the tarp that had been thrown over the body. As they were carrying away the dead man I began to wonder how the Vietnamese conduct funeral rites. None of the other Americans seemed to know either. But we were not long in finding out.

George got so irritated one afternoon a few days later that he almost broke his usual stride. It looked to him as if all the laborers were going on strike—or something just as viciously reprehensible—and for one whole day there would not be any work done in the yard. Not only that, they wanted to use the warehouse for what George described as "a goddamn voodoo banquet."

As far as I was able to make out, the Vietnamese believe that the spirit of the recently departed hangs about the place where he died and that his spirit might provide bad joss for the survivors unless it is appeased in the customary manner.

The funeral was a credit to Vietnamese sagacity and determination. The workers

A smart man takes his break where he can

narrowed down the likelihood of company refusal by waiting till the last minute to announce their intentions, in that way depriving the bosses of the time to organize resistance. As far as the laborers were concerned, the company's approval was a mere formality. The party that followed was nothing less than the feast they had planned.

There was a glistening suckling pig, apple and all, roast chickens, French bread stacked like fence pickets, great bowls of rice, dishes heaped with towering mounds of succulent fruit, pyramidal stacks of canned soups, and vegetables piled in great heaps as at the market stalls. The sight of all that food convinced me that we were

about to see an Oriental version of an Irish wake.

To guarantee that the spirit would have something with which to wash down the grand repast, the funeral committee had provided dozens of bottles of beer, soda, and Johnny Walker. For decoration there were fresh flowers and candles, and tiny banners on skewers had been stuck into the hide of the pig.

We were willing to bet that the dead man had never received so luxurious an honor during his lifetime. But now the violence of his death provided his spirit with the scepter of fear to command the lavish feast.

The ceremony itself was simple. Every

The funeral banquet

Vietnamese worker in the yard filed past the sacrificial commissary that morning. (In fact, there were a few faces that I'd never seen before. I suspected that they belonged to the workers who are said to go into hiding between paydays.) Each mourner performed the same supplication: hands held together, eyes raised toward heaven, a single clap of the hands, and down he would go on his knees for a long, deep bow with his arms outstretched before him.

We took to guessing what would follow the ritual. Someone suggested that the Vietnamese would probably douse the altar with gasoline and transform the offerings into a feast of soaring smoke, thus winning the satisfied spirit's everlasting blessing. There were nods of agreement and some of us looked about to see that the fire extinguishers were in their proper places.

But second guessing the Vietnamese is a hazardous enterprise. No one in that hungry crowd was about to turn all that good food into a flaming pyre. Not on your life!

Instead a forklift driver suddenly brought out a long wicked-looking knife, and every foreign spectator quickly took a step backward. While we nervously wondered how such a weapon was smuggled past the guards, the knife wielder unceremoniously stepped to the head of the table and began carving up the pig and passing out servings to all comers. Beer and soda bottle tops began popping, French bread was torn into bite-size pieces, canned goods were passed around and disappeared into gunny sacks, and the whole throng began happily chatting, laughing, and blowing out candles as though it were somebody's birthday.

The spirit, I supposed, was expected to make do with a spiritual repast. And if he was half as satisfied as the munching, grinning mourners, I had little doubt that when he had his fill he would depart for wherever Vietnamese spirits go and leave the living in peace.

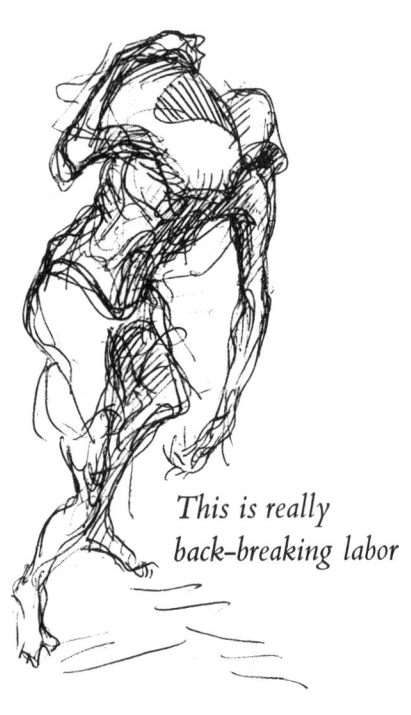

*This is really
back-breaking labor*

Women laborers funnel salvaged cement into bags

*What it means to be
really worn down*

Taking a betel-nut break

One thing that surprised me about some of our Vietnamese laborers was their evident willingness to squeal on each other. Once one of the men squealed to the foreman about a truck driver who was sleeping in a warehouse. The truck driver almost lost his job. It would probably have been better for the squealer if he had, because a few days later the truck driver lay in wait for him and laid him out with a two-by-four. I never found out what impression that made on the other men but I'm sure it impressed the squealer.

Waiting for the next load of cement

Streets of Saigon

A busy intersection near the Saigon Market

*Woman enjoying
a cup of coffee
at an outdoor cafe*

NEW SAIGON AND OLDTIMERS

THERE IS ALWAYS someone around to tell you—endlessly—about how good Saigon used to be. Surprisingly enough it isn't always the French oldtimer. (His chief complaint seems to be the GI's preference for pizza over bouillabaise.) No, it's the American businessman who is ever ready to bend your ear about the "good old days." The mortality rate for American businesses is high in Saigon, but always to be found—at your elbow in a bar most likely—is a businessman, or two, who can still remember the days of two-way traffic and the time when the city's garbage was almost manageable. These survivors of a happier age wax nostalgic over sweet vermouth at the hotel L'Admiral on Saturday afternoons and recall from a pleasure-filled past visions of delicate ladies strolling down the Rue d'Catinat, their lithe figures draped in flowing *ao dais* and their hair hip-length and glistening like a raven's wing. Through these visions no half-tracks clatter, no Hondas roar, and never of course do there appear the miniskirted, finger-snapping, gum-chewing, red-haired bar girls of the Tu Do bars.

Sad but true, the good old days of Saigon are gone forever—except in memory. The famous tree-lined boulevards of Saigon have been widened to provide maneuvering room for the trucks, jeeps, and Hondas that are crowding out the cyclos these days. The great trees have been cut down and made into furniture. The glazed-tile floors of the grand villas bear the marks of combat boots, the pastel-colored shutters are boarded up, the ceilings have been lowered, and the giant fans I have been scrapped to make way for air-conditioners that

Saigon's tree-lined boulevards were famous before they decided to widen them. Then many of the trees were cut down and made into decorator furniture.

drain the already inadequate power systems.

Touching though they may be, the sad tales of the oldtimers are not without irony. For the storytellers are the very entrepreneurs who contribute to the war effort such articles of trade as canned beer, swivel-type bar stools, stainless steel sinks, parboilers, barbecue cookers, pizza ovens, Ping Pong tables, formica-topped bars, and such other essentials as Granny Goose potato chips, Beanie Weenies, and beef jerky.

But the old Saigon certainly had a charm that the new lacks. Not so many years ago affluent Vietnamese and foreigners alike wheeled and dealed and sought and often found pleasure at the tables of the city's numerous sidewalk cafes. But then the introduction of air-conditioning lured some patrons indoors. Many others were driven off the terraces by the bomb-hurling

tactics of the terrorists. And, after a respectable passage of time, the hardy few who braved the heat and the threat of being blown to bits also deserted the outdoor tables. Some joined their friends because they could no longer bear to miss out on choice bits of gossip. Others, it was said, feared the gossipers' tongues more than the Cong's bombs. And still others were afraid they would not be talked about.

The new surroundings are undeniably safer but they are also gloomy and musty. And gone too is the simple pleasure of sitting quietly and gazing at the passing scene while sipping a refreshing drink.

But terrorists and modernity notwithstanding, the average Saigonese still seems to spend most of his day outdoors. And that is where you can find him today, much as I have recorded him in these pages.

The itinerant barber sets up "shop" wherever he finds a customer. His is a house-to-house business and scissors, razor, comb, and chair are the only license he needs. If he's a real go-getter, he'll also carry a portable awning of burlap to keep the sun off his customers. A jack-of-all-trades, the barber will also sharpen your kitchen knives and repair your broken fan.

The work of building, rebuilding, and repairing is endless here

Hand-drawn carts are still common on Saigon's streets

Sidewalk bicycle repairman fixing tire

Many women outpace the men

53

*If you can't find what
you want in the PX or
commissary, the chances
are it's on sale in
the black market*

THE BLACK MARKET

FOR THOSE DENIED the privilege of using the PX there's always the sidewalk vendor to fill your order for first-class merchandise. His blanket is usually covered with the same goods you'll find on exchange and commissary shelves. And, surprisingly, the open-air market will often carry a greater variety of Stateside sundries than the PX. The price he asks may even be cheaper, depending on how you get your piasters.

The Saigon black market fits exactly Mark Twain's description of the weather: Everybody talks about it but no one does anything about it. Does anything about doing away with it, that is. At least not anything with any lasting or important effect.

The black market fills a need. As every student knows, nature abhors a vacuum, and when the authorities failed to fill an important economic vacuum, the local en-

trepreneurs moved in with efficiency and enthusiasm. Supply meets demand with zest over the merchandise-covered blankets of the open-air market.

The black-market vendors soon learned to specialize, saving the shopper much confusion when he has something special in mind. Hardware, for example, seems to be the most popular merchandise on Nyugen Hue, at the stalls near the International House. On display you'll find measuring tapes, masking tapes, machines for making tapes, and of course, recording tapes. There are also tools too numerous to mention, from ordinary hammers, saws, and screwdrivers to power tools of every description. I never saw any computers, but before there are a half-dozen in the country, I will bet that at least one of them will make its scandalous way to the black-market stalls.

The plumbing department you'll find near the corner, between stationery and

dog food. The sports department is about two U.S. Army blankets up from the International House entrance. A recent sale there featured body-building equipment, complete with instruction booklets.

Down by the USO, Polaroid cameras are the big thing. Unfortunately the inner workings tend to be a bit rusty because the sidewalk clerks have yet to learn about stock rotation.

Scotch and brandy are popular items at back-street blankets. A word of warning though—the contents of the bottles tend to run to booze-colored tea. Countless hours of conjecture have been spent on just how the real stuff is emptied and replaced without breaking the seal on the bottle.

Any commodity in great demand is open to black-market exploitation. An example of this form of double-dealing is a product that was supposed to be a PX shipment of diarrhea-arresting Kaopectate, but which turned out to be curdled caraboa milk, something that aggravates the malady rather than cures it. One joker suggested that the real Kaopectate was used to paint the double white line that runs down the center of the Bien Hoa highway.

A walk in the black market usually irritates newcomer Americans. They get worked up over the corruption and profiteering evident in the sale of goods supposedly destined for GIs. What makes matters worse is that the sales are carried on blatantly, unashamedly. But indignation fades when suddenly a large can of V-8 is spotted—an item that hasn't been seen on a commissary shelf in God knows how long. The wary shopper tries to hide his joy and bargains for the can, to put it back to its intended use, supplementing an American breakfast. The stuff makes great Bloody Marys too. This way tolerance begins, and the black market gains another supporter.

When the only way to get your goods to market
is by hand cart, there's nothing to do but put
your back into your work, even if you know you're
going to end up like the man on the right

Even the black marketeers enjoy the afternoon siesta

Mealtime at a Saigon street stand

Sacred Heart Church, Cholon

Some women of Saigon

Driving in Saigon's traffic demands that my eye be quick enough to take in the young children chatting happily while the moons of their naked little bottoms are suspended over the curb, and still see in time the idiot on a bicycle who has just cut in front of me.

Lice search

Morning scene

Mother and child

Sedate bicyclist

The national gait is something to see. It's exaggerated almost to the level of caricature in women who are pregnant. Their bellies lead their stride, hips before chest, feet turned out, and arms swing loosely behind. That almost describes it, but you have to see it to believe it.

BEGGARS OF SAIGON

OLDTIMERS IN THE foreign community will tell you that begging is a way of life in the Orient, and professional beggars are common in Vietnam. The more than twenty-five years of war have produced refugees numbering in the tens of thousands and to no one's surprise a large number of these have had to turn to begging. In fact, beggars have become so common that both foreigners and the local people accept them as a fixed part of the city's character. Fixed or not, a walk down Tu Do any afternoon can be hazardous to the windowshopper, for he may run into some beggar's cart, trip over his kid, or step on his monkey. And if the shopper's sensitivities lie close to the surface, he will be forced to undergo some hideous shocks.

As you'd expect there is a large number of amputees among the beggars, and those without legs propel themselves along on wheeled platforms. There are also many

lepers among the beggars and these make their pitches by exposing their sores and moaning at passersby. House-to-house begging is a standard form, but the most common practice is to work the streets. Usually you'll hear an imploring cry and you'll find a conical hat or a small box thrust out before you by some pitiable old person.

Kids beg too and small children are sometimes used as a beggars' apprentices. While there are probably legitimate mothers here and there who have been reduced to beggary, the toothless old biddies carrying two-year-old babies are more than a little suspicious. I've been told that the most popular gimmick for panhandlers—especially old women tired of being fruit peddlers or water carriers—is to borrow a neighbor's small child, dirty him up a bit, and use him to gain added sympathy. However that may be, you can believe that the need of Saigon's beggars is real.

Lepers are not an uncommon sight in Vietnam, although getting used to them can be difficult. One man in particular caught and held my eye. He was often to be seen hunkering in the shade on a side street off Nyugen Hue and several times I came upon him as he was changing his bandages. He treated himself with Chinese salves purchased with money made by guarding parked cars against thieves and vandals.

Friday the 19th:
    Farmer: Hey, Dick, what's purple and illegal?
    Adair: I dunno.
    Farmer: Statutory grape.
Saturday the 20th:
    Farmer: Hey, Frankie, what's purple and illegal?
    Furci: An Indian money changer!

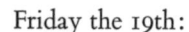

MAKING IT IN THE STREETS

To the ragged, barefoot kids—the war orphans and runaways—the streets of Saigon are home, school, and testing grounds. In narrow back alleys and on boulevard sidewalks these kids develop a cunning and a dedication to the art of simply surviving.

Watch Nguyen Qui. You'd better. A wiry eleven-year-old who can distract you with a broad, winning smile while he sells you yesterday's newspaper, flips the pen from your breast pocket, and shortchanges you, all in one flawless operation. He's skillful and he's fast. He has to be.

After a while it becomes a matter of your own survival, and you begin to think defensively. It becomes common sense to pay the driver before stepping out of the taxi because an exposed wallet is an easy snatch from Nguyen's level, and you'll pay hell trying to catch him. He knows every doorway and every alley in his turf and he moves out like a track star on his skinny brown legs. You may not like Nguyen—you'll probably hate him if he makes off with your watch or pen or camera—but you've got to respect him for coming out ahead against the odds.

Not long ago good fortune came to Nguyen Qui when he inherited a choice parking space on Nguyen Hue Street just opposite the U.S.O. The area was previously defended by an older fellow who moved up to a draftee's place behind a Tu Do street bar. When Nguyen sees you cruising about in your car, he'll give you

"I watch! I watch! I watch!"

the sign and direct you to his space. Then, before you turn off the ignition, he's at the window yelling, "I watch! I watch!"

What he means is that for a fee of from ten to fifty piasters he'll guard your car. He'll guard it from thieves and vandals. He's also guaranteeing that he won't let the air out of your tires or make off with your aerial or windshield wipers, which he'll do should you decide you don't require his services.

Be sure that what Nguyen's saying is "watch." After he's closed the deal for the protection job, he'll change his pitch to "Wash! Wash! Wash!" Keep your ears open. This is how he extends his services. What he's selling is a car wash; not the kind you get at your gas station back home, but

a quick once-over with a dirty, damp rag which supposedly rates an additional hundred piasters.

It was a shoeshine boy that put young Nguyen wise to the benefits of learning a few polite phrases in English. Nowadays when a customer pays him he responds with that rehearsed smile and says, "Thank you," as if he really means it. The gesture pays off not only in tips but in steady trade from familiar faces.

But should you consider yourself more worldly than young Nguyen and attempt to challenge him, whatever his ploy, he'll resort to his old tricks such as an up-yours gesture which will relieve you of any sentimental feelings should you consider a swift kick as proper response.

It takes many hours over the drawing board
to catch with mere pen and paper the lines
of the bones and clothes that emphasize the
cyclo driver's enervated slouch. But when
you next see him—perhaps as here, haggling
over a fare with an irate foreign woman—
you feel that you are seeing him truly for
the first time.

Hunkering, or squatting on the heels, is so common in Vietnam it might well be called the national posture. Look around you outdoors and at almost anytime you can see someone hunkering, usually in the shade. For one reason or another this time-honored Oriental practice has never been taken up seriously by Westerners. Even in Japan, which suffers from no shortage of rabid Japanophiles bent on saving all the old customs the Japanese are trying to shuck off, did I meet any foreign ascetics who practiced hunkering. Perhaps hunkering is not inscrutable enough.

The word "hunker" is believed to have come from the Scotch, though I never saw a Scotsman hunkering.

Wary old woman

74

Woman peddler

THE VIETNAMESE PACE

Except during curfew hours the streets are densely crowded. The tropical heat drives people out of the fiery interiors of houses and other buildings and is one of the reasons why in spite of the crowds you get a strange impression of inactivity or slow motion. Businessmen are dickering with customers on all sides, but the people seldom *look* busy. All around you see hundreds of people moving in that special way that reminds you of the ooze of heavy oil or a record being played too slowly. Or else they are just hunkering about in the shade digging the scenes through half-shut eyes, as though three-fourths of the population were on an opium high.

Some of the sluggishness is probably war-caused since thousands of people have been uprooted and forced into situations where they feel it's better to go slow than to rush into danger. But the general opinion has it that it's mostly just the Vietnamese way, that enervated slouch, the droopy expression, the stooped shoulders, and the torpid unwinding that ends in the characteristic squatting position.

Few Americans can slow themselves down to the Vietnamese pace. The local inertia sometimes gets on the nerves of the GIs, especially when it's accompanied by a smile of embarrassment, which is often misread.

As I sketched this kid sleeping in a doorway his head
kept bobbing, and several times he cracked it against
the stone framework. Surprisingly, he didn't appear
to be hurting himself because he kept dozing.

Lady bicyclist dressed in an ao dai

At the water pump

THE NEIGHBORHOOD PUMP

I once lived across the street from a public water pump.
Though the water ran constantly I cannot recall ever seeing it
run into the street. There was always a jug, jar, pan, or can
under the spigot, if not the body of a small child or somebody's
head. In spite of the burden borne by some of the very young
and very old women who lugged heavy water containers, I
think the women would greatly miss the activity and neighborhood gossip if they were suddenly given individual plumbing.

For an artist the public water pumps supply an endless
source of fascinating activity. There is the old woman with a
rag wrapped around her head who chews betel nut and hun-
kers over a large pan as she scrubs and wrings her laundry.

Water carriers

And there are naked children, fine in form and movement, who splash water and laugh and cry. Or there is a young teen-age girl, naked to the waist, working a lather into her long black hair, her head turned modestly sideways. Between rinses other women come and fill their water tins and walk away with that unforgettably comic swaying rhythm, the water containers bouncing at each end of a pole slung over their shoulders.

Some women come for water only two or three times a day, usually in the morning and again at night. They fill only their own containers. Others are at it all day, and these come and go in different directions. These busy women obviously make their living hauling water for others.

Street scenes: seven cops and two women

Cop checking a bicyclist's papers

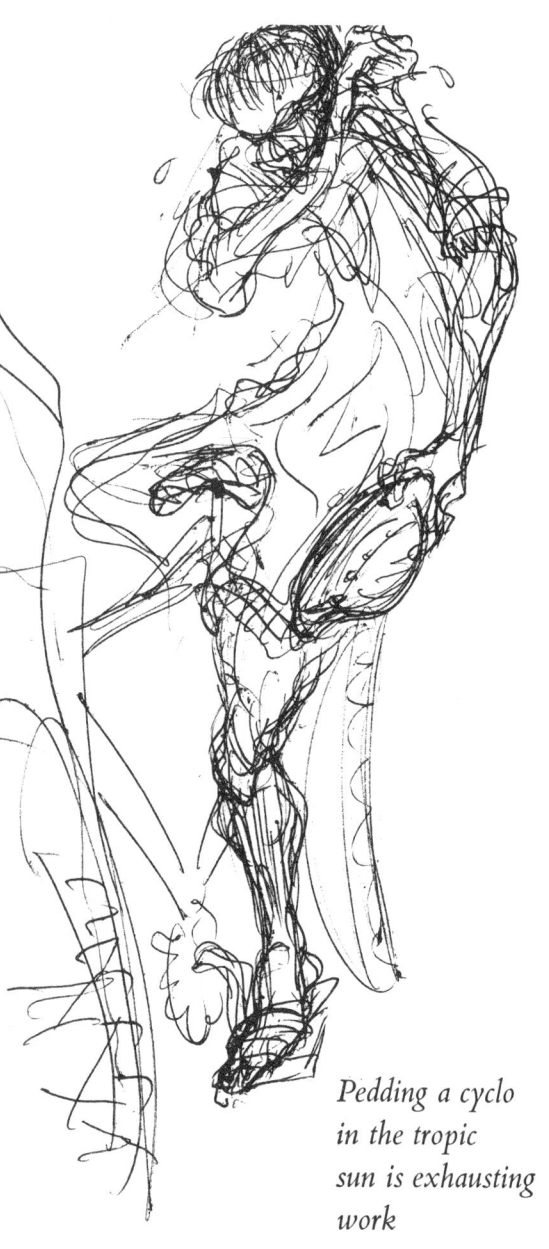

Pedding a cyclo
in the tropic
sun is exhausting
work

So is
carrying a
load like this

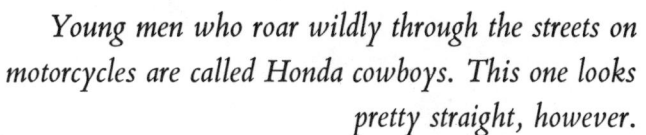

Young men who roar wildly through the streets on motorcycles are called Honda cowboys. This one looks pretty straight, however.

The food stands that are wheeled to the city's side streets each morning are busiest at breakfast and lunchtime. Popular staples of these traveling restaurants are a soup called *canh chua*, rice, and *cha gio* (fried fish or meat roll). Invariably the restaurateurs carry *nuoc mam*, a fermented fish sauce the smell of which no visitor to Vietnam ever forgets.

Outdoor cafe scenes, Saigon

Mess hall employees eating

I had finished lunch and was having a smoke at the NCO mess hall of the 1st Infantry Division at Di An. The Vietnamese mess workers had finished serving and were having their own lunch, the same fare the GIs eat. But they weren't eating it the way the GIs do. For instance, a pregnant woman at a nearby table had loaded her tray with huge helpings of mashed potatoes, peas and carrots, gravy, and spare ribs. Curiously, she did not separate the the food into the sections provided in the mess tray. Instead she heaped enough food for four people into one grand pile which she commenced to eat with a hearty appetite.

Security guard checking out military employees

A woman employee at work

Saigon Nights

When there were only about 4,000 American troops in Vietnam, it was the civilian workers who stood out in the streets of Saigon. They were impossible to miss in their field boots, gaudy aloha shirts, and easy-going manner as they stood in the lobby of the Star Hotel or outside on Tu Do street. They made good money and a lot of noise, and they were especially popular with the girls around the Windy Bar because they were free-spenders and treated their women well.

Bar scene

FEELING LONESOME

For the man who tires of spending his hard-earned piasters for thimbles of Saigon tea in return for reruns of the same dialogue in every bar, he need only pick up one of Saigon's English-language newspapers to discover that Miss Lee, Miss Lana, Miss Gina, et al., will only be too happy to supply him with a "friend" to exchange language and share his house, bed, and bankroll. He need never leave these agencies empty-handed for, as Miss Lee advertises, you can have a charming high-class young lady, a maid, or a car, or whatever else you need. It's all there under one roof.

Of course the classified columns also carry independent advertisers who feel they may have a better chance finding a man on their own by mentioning special assets such as their virginity and an apartment which they'll throw in with the deal. And some others are more selective; they require their man to be cultured, sober, Moslem, middle-aged, and well off. One determined "virgin lady" ran her ad daily for three weeks. I was so startled one day to find it missing that I was tempted to writer her a letter of congratulations. But then the ad showed up a couple of weeks later and she still billed herself "virgin lady."

Since it was Miss Lee's ad that I remembered as having the longest run (she even stayed open for business during the Tet Offensive), and because I was feeling lonesome I decided to give her services a try.

Miss Lee's villa stood just off a busy section of Cong Ly, one of Saigon's main streets. There were no signs. I guess she didn't anticipate much walk-in trade. The gate was open so I wandered towards the house and through an open doorway that led down a long hall. There wasn't a soul to be seen. Things were starting off badly. As a veteran of many a Saigon "tea" lounge, I fully expected to find the place bustling with lounging beauties waiting for me to size them up on my way to the administrative department. I didn't even see any of the little French cars Miss Lee's ad mentioned.

At last a girl of about six stuck her head out from behind a door. A little young I thought and began to wonder if this was the right place. Finally a slender middle-aged woman wearing an *ao dai* appeared and inquired, "Yes?"

"Well, I . . . uh, guess I'm looking for a girl . . . that is, if you're Miss Lee."

With a gesture of her hand I was told to follow. Miss Lee led me into a room furnished with a desk and three chairs. She opened a drawer and handed me a typewritten sheet which explained that I had three choices of ladies, in either language exchange, friendship, or marriage. The initial downpayment, should my application be accepted, was 500 piasters (a little over four dollars at the legal rate) which

Being introduced
at Miss Lee's agency

wouldn't be returned if I rejected all three. And 1500 piasters was payable on acceptance, slightly less for language exchange. Should I strike out, I could pay another 500 and play all over again. This could go on and on until Miss Lee ran out of girls, at which time I would be put on her mailing list at no extra charge.

"Do you understand the rules?" she asked.

"Yes ma'am, let's play ball!"

"You must first fill out this application. Our girls are very high-class and we must consider all applications very carefully before we make an introduction."

The application had three words: name, address, age. At the bottom I was to check the category I was interested in. I completed the form as best I could, and after Miss Lee studied it for a while she announced to my relief that it met her standards.

I had decided that friendship might be a good category to start with since marriage would have cost me an extra 250 piasters and a good friend might give me a little language on the side.

"How old?" she asked.

"Oh, not old, young . . . young!"

"How young?"

"Well, not too young," I replied, wondering if the six-year-old was waiting for a customer.

Miss Lee fingered through a large ring of keys and, unlocking another drawer, offered me an envelope containing about

*"My name Ngoc," she said again, still
studying the crack in the floor*

thirty photographs. There they were, the
lovely ladies I was looking for. In every
pose imaginable. Nice poses, mind you!
Oh, a few with bikinis, but mostly the
dramatic or glamor-type portraits you see
in every Saigon photo-shop window. Vietnamese ladies love to have their pictures
taken and the local photographers—in a
booming business—are quite skillful with
shadows, angles, and retouching. But because local hair styles are of a limited
variety, everybody pretty much looks like
everybody else in these pictures. Matter of
fact, there were a couple in the stack I
could have sworn I'd met someplace before.

Naturally they were all attractive, and
since the photos were supplied by the
ladies themselves, it was certain that each
reproduction only displayed the lady's
finest assets. Those wearing sweaters and
low-cut Western gowns seemed to be a
little fuzzy around the face. Of course I was

suspicious of dark shadows that might be
hiding a bad complexion or a few wrinkles,
and a foreshortened head shot was a dead
giveaway for a receding chin or a flat
nose. I could see that Miss Lee was becom-
ing impatient. She could have at least given
me a little hint as to which one, in her
opinion, might turn out to be a wild
friend.

It came down to a toss-up between the
sweet-looking girl in the *ao dai* with the
glassy faraway look in her eyes and the
cute tilt to her head, and the girl whose
ears stuck out and had big knockers. I
finally decided on the one with the tilted
head because she might be less resistant if
sometime I was feeling very friendly and
she wasn't feeling so friendly.

Miss Lee said her name was Miss Ngoc
and that she was, of course, very high-class.
Miss Lee would contact Miss Ngoc and she
would be introduced to me the following
morning right there in the office. Then I

would have to make up my mind whether or not I wanted Miss Ngoc to be my friend.

I arrived a little early the next morning. Miss Lee was talking to another customer, a fiftyish-looking army major. He looked pretty serious. Probably here to pick a wife, I thought. But maybe he just wanted to look at some pictures of cars or maids. Anyway, I was wishing he'd make up his mind and leave. I didn't want a bunch of people standing around distracting Miss Ngoc's glassy faraway look.

The major was still there when Miss Ngoc arrived, her face hidden by a small silk parasol which she persistently kept between us as if I might give her sunburn. At last Miss Lee looked up and said, "This is Miss Ngoc. Do you like her?"

Like her? I couldn't even see her. Maybe the parasol was part of the ceremony and if I could get her to drop it she'd have to be my friend.

"Well, couldn't we talk or something first?" I pleaded.

Miss Lee gestured towards the two empty chairs then returned to the major's problem. Having received Miss Lee's nod of approval, Miss Ngoc finally abandoned her parasol, sat down, and proceeded to contemplate a crack in the floor.

Seating myself opposite her I broke the silence. "Do you speak English?" I ventured.

"My name Ngoc," she replied.

"Yes, I know. Would you like to be my friend?"

"My name Ngoc," she repeated, still studying the crack.

"Would you like some gum?" I tried. I felt I was finally making progress.

"You're very pretty," I said, feeling bolder.

"My name Ngoc." She spoke with gum in her mouth.

I recall there being a long silence at this point and I had become rather fascinated by that crack in the floor myself. The major must have sensed my embarrassment, and having been relieved as the center of attention, he used the opportunity to excuse himself by saying he'd think the deal over.

"What do you think about Miss Ngoc?" Miss Lee persisted.

"I think she is a very pretty girl. I think, that is, I guess." Actually it was pretty hard to tell with her always looking down and her long black hair as good concealment as her parasol.

"Why don't you take her someplace for tea?" offered Miss Lee.

"Would you like some tea, Miss Ngoc?"

No answer. She had slipped off one shoe and was now following the crack with her big toe.

"I think we're having a communication problem, Miss Lee." What I really wanted to do was forget the whole thing. I thought I might pay my fee and buy Miss Ngoc a cup of tea just to get out of the thing. But then the girl would have probably been taken off Miss Lee's list and she never would find a friend or whatever. Then again, I thought, maybe it's all a gag. Maybe they're just putting me on. Maybe it's a racket and Miss Ngoc just goes around playing dumb and splitting the settlement with Miss Lee. You can see I was getting desperate.

"Miss Ngoc is a high-class girl and she is very shy," said Miss Lee. "But you must make up your mind."

"Uh, Miss Ngoc, maybe you'd rather exchange language?" I offered. "You don't have to be my friend if you don't want to."

She giggled.

"Miss Ngoc, what would you like to do?" I finally pleaded.

"I go toilet." Miss Ngoc slipped back into her shoe, arose, said something to Miss Lee in Vietnamese, and scurried down the hall.

"Miss Lee," I begged, taking advantage of the respite, "I don't want to hurt this nice girl's feelings but I really think she's maybe too high-class for me."

Miss Lee was understanding. She picked up Miss Ngoc's parasol and joined her in the toilet. A few minutes later I saw the parasol pass by my door and out of the house.

Miss Lee returned with her keys in hand and started for the picture drawer. I couldn't go through that again! There may not have been anything in the rules about chickening out after the first strike, but anyway Miss Lee was happy to make some adjustments.

After some negotiations I settled for a cute little Renault Dauphine with a slightly dimpled fender. We lived together one month when she began dripping oil on my driveway. But we parted good friends.

Bar girl

Experience showed that sketching in bars is good for learning concentration. It's also a good form of protection against VD, if the artist can keep his mind on his work.

CAT-PHUONG
TAILLEUR
SPORT BAR
STEAM BATH
MASSAGE

95

The Sporting Bar on Tu Do

*Letting it all hang
out, Saigon style*

"You buy me Saigon tea?"

Dancing couples, before the Tet Offensive

*When there are no
partners you can
always dance alone*

Bar girls, lookout kid, and beggar waiting for
customers in front of a Tu Do street bar

Inside, the same bar may look like this

Many nights I go to the Flamingo Bar, walk in feeling good and hoping for a little warmth from the girls because I'm a regular customer. As always though what greets me is blank stares, except from Lily, the mama-san. She recognizes all her customers. About the time I'm downing my second drink, I remember that I've seen all these deadpan women before and as always I notice with disgust the dingy walls, cracked plaster, non-flushing toilet, ice being chopped and tiny pieces flying in the customers' faces, and the bar boys hustling us by removing unfinished drinks of Saigon tea from the tables.

But why expect anything different? It's no different elsewhere on Tu Do. A promise means nothing here where the girls take your money, duck out the back door, and ride off on a scooter.

MPs making a curfew check in a bar— "Mais oui, I am French, monsieur!"

*After a certain point
living it up becomes
living it down*

Up until the time the American embassy officials decided that all U.S. citizens in Saigon would henceforth come under their control, we civilians enjoyed the privilege of staying out an hour later than the GIs. When the law went into effect, bar checks by MPs would begin about 10 p.m., a time when, as every member of saloon society knows, the action picks up. The bar owners counterattacked by placing a little kid as lookout at the open door. When he spotted the MPs coming, the kid would give the alarm, which sent various ranks and occupations into the toilet or down on the floor behind the bar.

Letting my hair grow and pretending to be French nearly freed me from the embassy's curfew restrictions. When an MP would asked me for my I.D. card, I'd raise my hands, shrug my shoulders in my best French manner, and make a questioning grunt through my nose. Eventually a situation developed in which the phony Frenchmen outnumbered the real ones.

The customer likes to pass his time playing around with the bar girls. Once he's confident he's won her over, he expects the girl of his choice to play straight with him. When she agrees to meet him after work he expects that, barring unforeseen emergencies, she'll be there. After all, who would believe a young woman would be as callow (and as careless) as to tell an out-and-out lie and ditch a man without expecting some kind of retribution? But believe it or not they do just that. Which is why, I suppose, so many girls get clouted in Tu Do bars.

RANDOM OBSERVATIONS ON VIETNAMESE WOMEN

Whoever it was that decided that the Vietnamese were capable of both defending and governing themselves must have drawn his inspiration from observing the women. For unlike many of her Asian counterparts, the Vietnamese woman does not customarily take a back seat in family or business affairs.

Bitter experience taught me that a man can find no more formidable adversary than a pregnant landlady, especially one backed up by a sister or cousin in the same condition. Her social status plus her prominent belly are considered so important that she does not deign to call her husband into negotiations. Who needs a mere man?

A Vietnamese woman is sentimental, emotional in the extreme, and seldom logical. To negotiate on her property is a disaster since the disputant's essential advantage lies not in value or right but on whose ground the dispute takes place.

The same woman places a high value on her sexual allure and though, as elsewhere, kind words and a charming manner may help you win the lady, you can bet your last dollar that the contract will only be con-

Bar girl

summated with the exchange of money. Kept women and wives expect the man to provide them with a regular monthly allotment that is commensurate with *their* idea of their status. While in America, at least, money is hardly the highest proof of love, in Vietnam the rule is no money no love. So, romantic souls and Cheap Charlies be warned, not only will you miss out on the fun but you also run the risk of bodily harm. Because impulsive behavior is the norm. No bar girl, for example, reasons about picking up a bottle of 33 beer and slamming it over the head of the Cheap Charlie who refuses to buy her a Saigon tea; she just does it. Likewise a "nice" girl never intends to lose her temper. But both, it seems, are easily provoked, and if you insist on going into detail about why you feel a lady is not worth the money she expects you to lavish on her, she may very well close the discussion with that handy beer bottle. The lady of class will make do with a bottle of PX catsup, however.

Carrying water is a hard job for any woman

*Vietnamese women
are tough and not
easily put down*

Sometimes the customers are in the mood for action . . .

. . . but more often they've got other diversions on their minds

Bar scene

Another sucker going for the bait

*Homely bar girl sitting alone. Maybe she's wondering if
she'd have done better back home on the farm.*

There is no end to being
hustled in a Saigon bar,
and even kids get into the act

The War

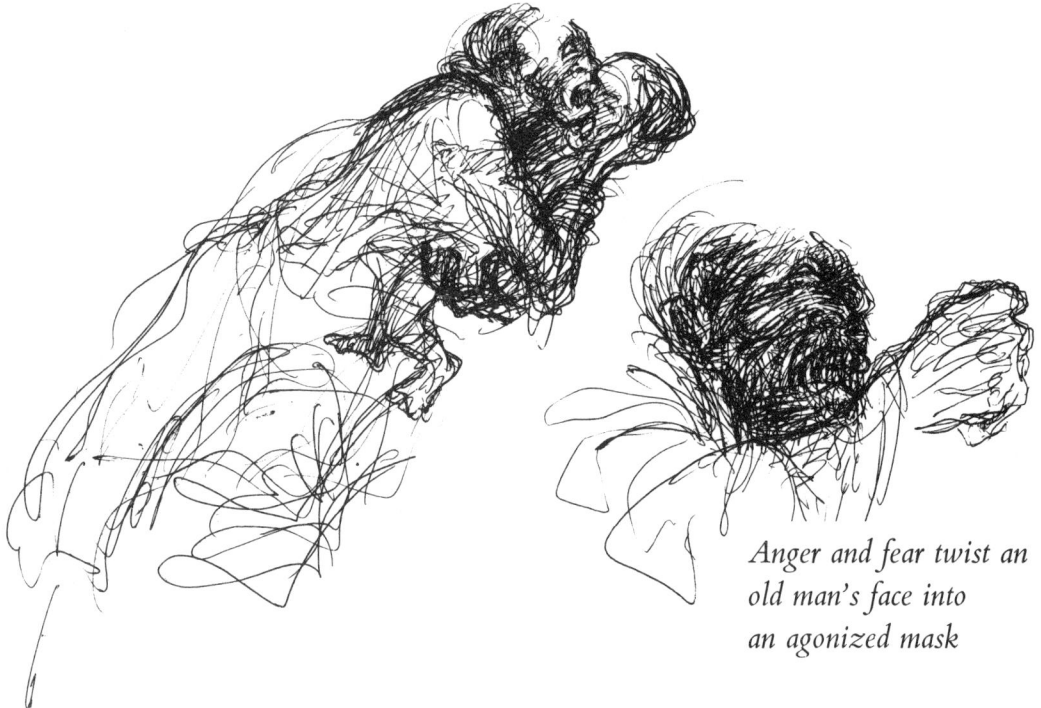

Anger and fear twist an old man's face into an agonized mask

Frightened woman runs from Viet Cong

THE TET OFFENSIVE

IF THE MAID says "beaucoup boom-boom" once more I'm going to have her boiled in *nuoc mam!* But then why shouldn't she bitch? She risks sneaking home to Cholon every night, when all Vietnamese are supposed to be off the streets, and makes it back the next morning with eggs for breakfast and chicken for lunch. We're lucky. A lot of my neighbors are living on C-rations. But I suspect a few of them are also being supplied by Ah Foon, my Chinese-Vietnamese chicken-running maid, who has an uncanny talent for discovering new sources of revenue.

All day long planes and helicopters drone over the city. There is sporadic shooting in the streets, especially at roadblocks and at barricades where nervous cops challenge everybody by firing into the air. All business has shut down.

Doherty got drunk and passed out on the floor last night. That's not unusual, though. He's been sleeping there every night since the offensive began. This afternoon, after a week of unsuccessful attempts to get home, he finally made it past the barricades and stayed long enough to pick up a bottle of Black Label and a six-pack of tamales and beans, which should spice up the chicken a bit.

Most of the foreign civilians have armed themselves with rifles, shotguns, or re-

"They're destroying everything!"

volvers. Jim Galagan has a continual Monopoly game going on at his place. They're using real money and Jim is enjoying being the grand host and banker. His pantry is well stocked and his gourmet stomach is suffering only from the .45 wedged into his belt. Rumors and lack of information have put everybody on edge. And with the booze and the boredom the Monopoly game sometimes gets out of hand. Galagan's wife locked herself in her bedroom during one session, and wouldn't come out till Tom Welsh agreed to sell her the B&O Railroad.

Armed Forces radio and T.V. keep repeating kill ratios and football scores with little information other than what they siphon off the wire services. Inside people are watching "Combat" while outside Viet Cong snipers are firing in the streets. The radio occasionally announces that curfew is still in effect and orders everybody to stay in their billets. Doherty figures that if Ah Foon is intrepid enough to sneak into Cholon for a chicken one of us ought to be able to make it down to the Flamingo Bar to liberate a couple of girls. I tell him that for the moment I am satisfied with the Scotch and tamales.

Everything is taking on an exaggerated importance. It even makes me nervous watching the doomed chickens as they

Soldier directing civilians to safety during Tet fighting

Terror in the streets

Man fleeing Viet Cong

cluck and scratch up and down the driveway all morning waiting for me to pass sentence. Fortunately our lights haven't gone out yet. The V.C. have been harassing the power stations and a lot of people are playing Monopoly by candlelight. Since we have to conserve what butane is left for cooking, we don't have hot water for baths, a small inconvenience at this time, but we're wondering how far this will go.

* * *

Only a few days ago Norm Kurtz and I started out in our little Renault for Long Binh Post, the sprawling U.S. military base twenty miles up the heavily traveled Bien Hoa Highway. The news from the Armed Forces Radio was that the V.C. had unsuccessfully tried to take over the U.S. Embassy in Saigon earlier that morning. If we had been able to understand the Vietnamese broadcasts or if we had been more concerned about Ah Foon's not showing up for breakfast that morning, we might have guessed that the attack was more than an isolated incident.

Just past Saigon's Dakow intersection we noticed the local police stopping Vietnamese pedestrians. Further down the road all traffic was stopped. A Lambretta scooter was overturned and people had gathered around what appeared to be a body. We figured it was just another traffic accident, common enough on this stretch of the highway. No one stopped us and we drove on past.

The Gia Dinh intersection is usually bustling with traffic. As we neared it, Norm, who was driving, mentioned how strange it was that the crossing was deserted. There were vehicles, plenty of them, but no drivers. It wasn't just strange; it was frightening. Norm had cautiously let up on the accelerator and we were slowly passing abandoned cars, trucks, and jeeps and not a soul was in sight.

It was at the crossing, under the signal, that we saw an overturned jeep and several dead ARVN soldiers lying in the road. Impulsively Kurtz hit the brakes—forgetting to use the clutch—we skidded and stalled, stopping in a pool of blood. Both of us

Combat police manning a checkpoint

119

Like this man, many people risked gunfire and flames to save their possessions

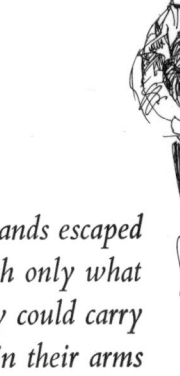

*Thousands escaped
with only what
they could carry
in their arms*

*The usually lethargic Vietnamese
became intensely animated by
the fighting in the city*

froze as if not wanting to interupt the stillness. A shot rang out, a sharp carbine staccato that never stopped echoing. I cracked my head on the dashboard trying to dive between my legs. Kurtz's head was next to mine although most of him was still on the seat, his fingers white from forcing the starter button. The engine roared with the grind of gears, Kurtz jumped the clutch, and we began to slide all over the wet pavement. Frantically we both tore at the wheel trying to control the spinning automobile. There may have been another shot. I don't know. All I remember is a great pounding in my ears. Kurtz and I must have both been yelling. As if in gruesome response, our rear wheels collided with an ARVN corpse giving us the traction we needed. We shot out onto dry road passing over the legs of another soldier. Heading in the direction of Saigon, Kurtz floored the gas pedal and didn't let up till we came to the Dakow roadblock. We were waved on through, but other cars, including those heading in the direction we had just come from, were stopped and the

Vietnamese drivers made to get out with hands in the air. Why the hell didn't they stop *us* when we were headed that way? Our fright had turned to anger considering the times the Vietnamese police hadn't hesitated to stop us for some small infraction of their complicated traffic regulations as an excuse to squeeze a few piasters out of us. But that morning we were as dispensable as the nineteen other American civilians who, we later learned, had been killed that day. We drove very slowly back down Phan Thanh Gian and could see the sky black with smoke over Cholon, something we had failed to notice earlier while driving out of the city.

*   *   *

Ah Foon is shaking her head and shrugging her shoulders in the French gesture for frustration. We've run out of butane, which will give the chicken a short reprieve. But lunch will be served as usual. Our enterprising Ah Foon has swapped the chicken for a good supply of C-rations.

Civilians running to escape being caught between friendly and enemy fire

Many civilians did not get away in time

Civilians fleeing a danger zone in Cholon

Cholon street fighting

Young women preparing a meal in Cholon war ruins

127

Buddhist monks, halted
in their demonstration
march by government troops,
sit and wait for orders
from their leaders

Buddhist monks sitting
behind barbed-wire barricade

In May 1966 the militant Buddhists again tried to bring down the Saigon government. They assembled their followers and marched from the Vien Hoa Dao Buddhist Center down Phan Dinh Phung and headed toward the American embassy. But at Le Van Duyet they were stopped by President Ky's National Police with barbed wire and tear gas. They waited for several hours at the barricades, many sitting in the cross-legged lotus position, their faces streaked with tears, singing and chanting prayers while Ky's police retaliated with rock music blasted through loudspeakers.

It wasn't long before the monks and their followers took their defiance to the streets. They painted slogans on the pavements and ran wild in the streets. Some people moved their family altars from their homes and set them on tables in the middle of the boulevards. Others turned over wooden carts and used them as barricades.

Since any kind of disturbance brings out bands of kids, they turned up everywhere, helping to stop traffic, throwing rocks, turning over vehicles, and setting them on fire. For the kids it was a grand holiday, but for the Buddhists, who had helped bring down five governments, it was the end of their bid for political power. President Ky outwitted their leaders and internal dissension split their ranks soon after.

Buddhist monk demonstrator

Monks and their followers set up altars
in the streets knowing that
government convoys would not
try to force their way through

A South Vietnamese soldier stands guard over demonstrating Buddhist opponents of the government

THE SITUATION AT PHU LOI

As I looked out the window of the main officers' club in Phu Loi, I could see the first choppers returning from a skirmish just this side of the Cambodian border. The MEDEVAC choppers landed first to unload the wounded, and were followed by UH-1 troop carriers while giant Chinooks hovered overhead, crippled choppers dangling from their slings. The ambush must have been as bad as everybody suspected.

The little one-and-a-half-ton air-conditioner in the club conference room groaned and sputtered and the fluorescent lights blinked as the power continuously fluctuated. There were beads of sweat on the major's face as he laid out the crude floor plan.

"Now what we had in mind, Mr. Adair, was to rip out this wall and extend the kitchen into what is now the latrine so that we might accommodate the new pizza oven and soft-drink dispenser."

The Chinooks were now delicately unloading their mangled cargo in a grassy area to the side of the landing zone, reeling in their slings, and turning back in the direction they had come from.

"If we eliminate this one section of bar where the formica is cracked anyway," the major continued, "we'd have room for another table."

"Or another slot machine," the sergeant-custodian suggested.

The wounded, some on stretchers, some walking, were being loaded onto deuce-and-a-half trucks. Fresh troops were climbing into the "slicks," as the troop carriers are called.

"I think we have enough slot machines already, sergeant."

"Another quarter machine would make twice as much as that table, sir, even if it was full all the time," the sergeant persisted.

"Another table, sergeant, would, I'm sure, be more consistent with the decor of the club. Don't you think so, Mr. Adair?"

Christ, I was thinking, if I could only get out there for ten minutes and sketch those guys getting off the choppers. Even if I could only get their gear all piled up next to the truck where the wounded are being loaded. What a great ink sketch that'd make. Maybe if I take out my pad and pretend to be making some notes I can get the gesture of that. . . .

"Mr. Adair? I asked what you think?"

"I think we'd better talk to the medics, major," I answered still looking out the window.

"The medics?"

"Yes."

"About a table?"

"No, about the latrine." I turned away from the window and faced the major. The room seemed very dark after staring out the window. "If you move the latrine I guess you know you must have the medic's

U.S. troops jump from helicopter and hit the ground on the run

approval for its new location. Are you using a septic tank for the present latrine or a cesspool?"

"Are we using a septic tank or a cesspool now, sergeant?"

"What's the difference between a septic tank and a cesspool?" the sergeant wanted to know, and I suspected the major did too.

"Well, one has to be pumped out periodically and the other drains out from a tank after being chemically dissipated." Let them find out which is which on their own, I thought.

"I think they pump this one," the sergeant offered after some consideration. "Cause there's this here truck that comes around every once in a while from town and it sure stinks the place to high heaven."

"Major, if you can find out exactly where the new latrine can be situated I'll be happy to come back and offer an estimate. In the meantime if the helicopter is ready I'd like to get back to Saigon before dark."

"I'll have all that information for you, Mr. Adair. As I mentioned before, the colonel considers this a rush project, with all the new personnel coming in." The major was very cooperative. "By the way, what do you think about that table?"

"If I get the toilet contract along with the extended kitchen and the order for a new pizza oven, I'll throw in the table for nothing. . . . Sorry, sarge!"

U.S. gunner wrapped
in ammo belts

Troops of the 3rd Brigade, 4th Division take
a break at Ban Me Thuot airstrip

Suspected Viet Cong
awaiting interrogation

*Sp/4 Mike Farris of Detroit,
Michigan, on guard duty in
the Duc Lap "Crows' Nest"*

*Pfc Tom Grace of
Foglan, Oklahoma,
plays with the child
of a wounded CIDG*

*A young soldier of
the Duc Lap CIDG*

When I finally got an assignment as an artist–correspondent for *Stars & Stripes*, one of the places I visited was a desolate area called Duc Lap. There I sketched the men of a Civilian Irregular Defense Group (CIDGs). The unit was made up of Vietnamese, Montagnards, and Cambodians who took their work seriously and looked to be ready for anything. Assigned to the Duc Lap unit as advisers were twelve Green Berets.

Inside the team shack

CIDG troops in formation. Minimum age is fourteen

CIDG sentry keeps vigiliance in a mortar pit

CIDG family in front of their bunker "home"

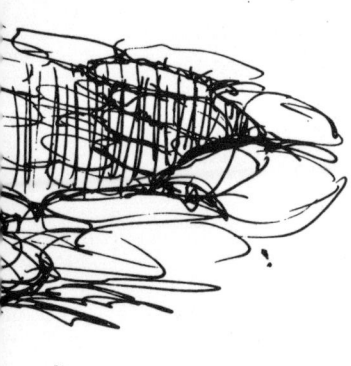

M/Sgt Nguyen Dinh Thang
marks tooth number on
a patient's hand

EPILOGUE

In 1965 I arrived at the Port of Saigon, and like a lot of the materiel off-loaded in those days, got sidetracked by the promoters and prof-iteers, became part of the economy—much the same as a can of black-market V-8 juice does. Eventually though I made it into the field, where I had originally consigned myself. The process took nearly five years, but my involvement in the life of Saigon was far better than any as-signment I could have planned. As an uninvolved spectator I could never have gathered the rich store of impressions I now carry, those of Saigon as it really is. My only regret is not having been able to sketch a day like that which will come when all the wrought-iron balconies will be draped with garlands of jasmine and when the women will throw flowers to the cheering crowd in the streets—the day when peace will come to Saigon and all Vietnam.

Viet Cong prisoner

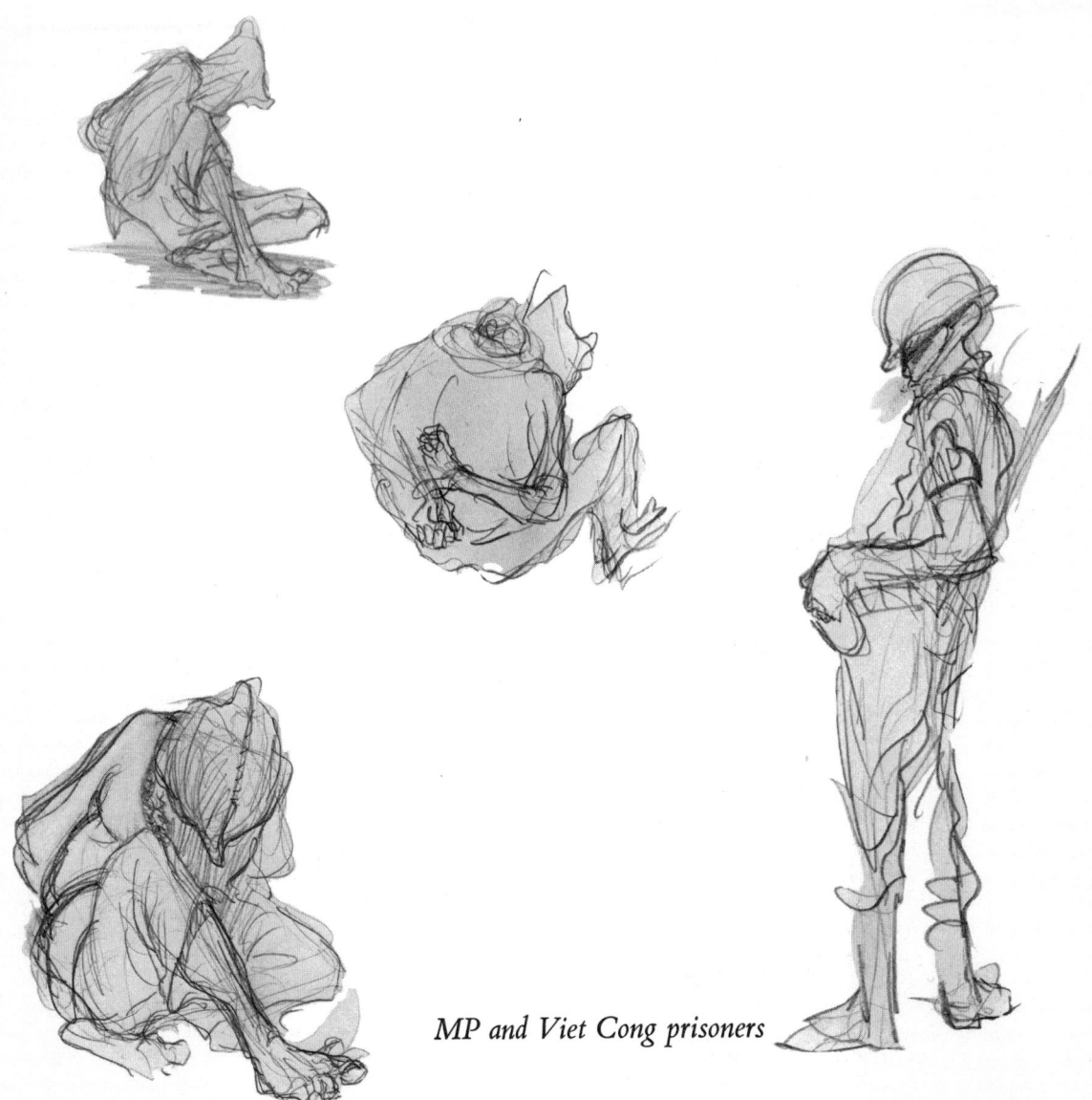

MP and Viet Cong prisoners

The "weathermark" identifies this book as having been planned, designed, and produced at John Weatherhill, Inc., 7-6-13 Roppongi, Minato-ku, Tokyo. Book design, layout, and typography by Ronald Bell. Composition by General Printing Co., Yokohama. Platemaking and printing by Kinmei Printing Co., Tokyo. Bound at the Makoto Binderies, Tokyo. The main text is set in 11-pt. Monotype Bembo, with hand-set Perpetua for display.